Cover illustration: MCV80, the Warrior Platoon Vehicle, under-going trials on Salisbury Plain. (Author)

1. The Carrier, Maintenance, Full Tracked FV434 is employed by the Royal Electrical and Mechanical Engineers (REME) for the repair and maintenance of AFVs in the field such as these Chieftain Main Battle Tanks.

TANKS ILLUSTRATED No 23

British Combat Vehicles Today

SIMON DUNSTAN

a&ap

ARMS AND ARMOUR PRESS

Published in 1986 by Arms & Armour Press Ltd.,
2–6 Hampstead High Street, London NW3 1QQ.

Distributed in the United States by Sterling
Publishing Co. Inc., 2 Park Avenue, New York,
N.Y. 10016.

British Library Cataloguing in Publication Data:
Dunstan, Simon
British army combat vehicles today. –
(Tanks illustrated; 23)
1. Armored vehicles, Military – Great
Britain
I. Title   II. Series
623.74′75′0941   UG446.5

ISBN 0-85368-777-3

Editing, design and artwork by Roger Chesneau.
Typesetting by Typesetters (Birmingham) Ltd.
Printed and bound in Italy by GEA/GEP in
association with Keats European Ltd., London.

To Kevin and his Pig

Introduction

The importance of logistic and combat support vehicles to a modern, mechanized army cannot be overstated. On the battlefield, the firepower of the main battle tank and the mobility of the infantry fighting vehicle are but naught without the basic prerequisites of ammunition and fuel as well as a multitude of other items needed to sustain the fighting soldier and his weapons.

Whether, as in the Falklands War, the logistic train is 8,000 miles from the home base to the war zone or thirty miles from San Carlos to the hills overlooking Port Stanley, the smooth passage of *matériel* to the front line is essential to the prosecution of warfare. The method of moving such supplies requires many different forms of transport, from the largest aircraft to the workaday truck. Equally important are the combat support vehicles, without which neither fighting nor transport vehicles could manoeuvre around the battlefield; conversely, their ability to impede an enemy's mobility is also a vital task.

British Army Combat Vehicles Today illustrates the diverse range of equipment in general service that fulfils these roles. Unless otherwise noted, all the photographs are reproduced by courtesy of the Ministry of Defence Public Relations departments, to whom I extend my thanks, as I do to GKN Sankey Defence Operations.

Simon Dunstan

◀2
2. The FV432 forms the basis for a number of special-purpose variants, including this FV439 Royal Signals Vehicle attached to the 1st Battalion, The Prince of Wales's Own Regiment of Yorkshire, seen moving out of a wood during Exercise 'Red Rat 74' in Germany.

▲3 ▼4

04 BT 58

3. Warrior, the latest British Army AFV for the infantry, churns up the mud during troop trials. Designated MCV80 (Mechanized Combat Vehicle of the '80s), it forms the basis of a complete family of medium tracked military vehicles. (GKN Sankey)

4. A prototype MCV80 goes through its paces during mobility trials at Bovington. Warrior is powered by a 550hp Rolls-Royce CV8CA V8 engine coupled to an Allison X Series cross-drive transmission system, giving a high power-to-weight ratio. (Author)

5. The MCV80 can carry up to ten men, including commander and driver. It fulfils the stringent requirements of modern mechanized infantry to operate in the demanding conditions of the 48-hour battlefield scenario. (Author)

6. The Rolls-Royce Condor engine and Allison transmission are situated in the right front of the vehicle, beside the driver. This combination is conservatively rated to reduce fuel and maintenance costs while providing a range of over 400 miles. (Author)

6 ▼

▲7 ▼8

7. The hull of MCV80 is of all-welded aluminium alloy construction, giving greatly increased protection and levels of mobility over its predecessor, the FV432 APC. (Author)

8. Warrior is due to enter service with the British Army in 1987 and will supplement the FV432 APC rather than replace it on a one-to-one basis. (Author)

9. The British Army has a requirement for 1,048 Warriors, which are to be built by GKN Sankey Defence Operations in Shropshire. Seventy per cent will be Platoon Vehicles and the remainder specialized support vehicles. (Author)

10. The first three variants will be command, artillery observation and combined repair and recovery vehicles. The vehicle illustrated is configured in the command role for trials purposes. (Author)

11. Warrior has a crew of two, comprising driver and gunner. In the troop compartment there are seven seats (one of which is a commode) for the infantry section, whose leader also acts as vehicle commander. (Author)

9▲

10▲ 11▼

12. With its combination of a 30mm Rarden cannon and a coaxial 7.62mm Hughes Helicopters Ex-34 Chain Gun, mounted in its two-man steel turret, the MCV80 Platoon Vehicle has considerable firepower. The boxes on each side of the mantlet contain the Visual and Infra-Red Screening Smoke System (VIRSS) as a protection against modern surveillance and target acquisition devices such as thermal imagers. (Author)

13. Access to the troop compartment is via the twin doors in the rear of the hull, with double roof hatches above. Unlike several contemporary infantry combat vehicles, Warrior has no provision for the troops to fire their small arms from inside. (Author)

14. The combination of aluminium alloy armour, a powerful Rolls-Royce engine and an advanced suspension system gives Warrior high acceleration and mobility over all types of terrain as well as short exposure time from cover to cover, so substantially reducing the chances of enemy hits. Here, a Warrior Platoon Vehicle moves across country in company with its predecessor, the FV432 APC. (Author)

15. A Warrior engages a target during firing trials. MCV80 weighs 24 tonnes and has a maximum road speed of 75km/h. (GKN Sankey)

▲16 ▼17

12

18▲

◀19

16. Less sophisticated (and considerably less expensive) than the Warrior MCV80 is the Saxon, which is in service with the British Army as an APC for non-tracked infantry battalions. (GKN Sankey)

17. Unlike many contemporary and often unreliable AFV designs, Saxon combines simplicity of concept and operation with flexibility of role, capacity and protection, making it a cost-effective solution to meet many different operational requirements. (Author)

18. Saxon has ample room for a crew of two (comprising driver and commander) plus nine infantrymen, as well as stowage space for weapons, two days' combat supplies and additional ammunition. (Author)

19. The APC is powered by a GM Bedford Type 500 six-cylinder diesel engine; the transmission and other automotive components are also standard commercial items, thus reducing procurement and running costs. (Author)

20. (Next spread) Saxon is now in widespread service with the British Army and has been sold to five other countries. A number of variants are currently available, including a recovery model and an ambulance, which are shown here following a standard APC. (GKN Sankey)

▲21 ▼22

21. Saxon has an all-terrain capability, with large tyres for maximum footprint to reduce ground pressure. The transfer gearbox offers two- or four-wheel drive in high or low ratios, giving good traction and gradient-climbing performance. (GKN Sankey)

22. The Saxon provides crew protection against small-arms ball and AP rounds, against 155mm HE artillery air bursts and, on account of the 'V'-shaped configuration of the hull, against anti-tank mines up to 9kg. (GKN Sankey)

23. The predecessor of the Warrior MCV is the FV432 APC (Armoured Personnel Carrier), which evolved from the long line of Bren and Universal Carriers of Second World War fame. Here, riflemen deploy from an FV432 Mk 2 during a training exercise.

24. An FV432 Mk 1 APC crosses a No. 9 Tank Bridge during exercises with the 1st Cheshire Battle Group at the British Army Training Unit, Suffield, Canada. The FV432 Mk 1 can be distinguished by the exhaust pipe mounted on the roof.

25. Crashing through a forest in Germany, an FV432 Mk 2 of the 2nd Battalion, Royal Irish Rangers, participates in Exercise 'Swordthrust'. This 432 mounts an enclosed Peak Engineering 7.62mm machine gun turret.

26. An FV432 Mk 2 APC of the 1st Battalion, Scots Guards, undergoes training in Germany. Note the NBC filter pack housing on the right-hand side of the hull, which is more compact and protrudes less than that fitted to the Mk 1.

27. The 4,000 soldiers, 18 helicopters and over 550 AFVs of the British Army of the Rhine which took part in a Royal Review at Sennelager in July 1977 to mark the Silver Jubilee of Her Majesty Queen Elizabeth II represented the largest parade of armour ever held by the British Army. Seen here are FV432 APCs, with a Gazelle helicopter and M107 175mm self-propelled guns in the background.

28. The Launcher, Guided Missile, Carrier Mounted, Full Tracked, Swingfire, FV438 is the tank-destroyer version of FV432. It is capable of knocking out hostile MBTs and AFVs at a distance of 4,000m.

▲25   ▼26

▲29 ▼30

29. The FV438 has two launchers mounted on the rear hull roof which are loaded from inside the vehicle, where an additional fourteen Swingfire wire-guided missiles are stored.
30. A number of FV432 APCs have been fitted with the same 30mm Rarden cannon-armed turret as the CVR(T) Scimitar and CVR(W) Fox armoured car, to give an effective APC- or MICV-killing capability.
31. Medics of an FV432 Armoured Ambulance of 7 Field

Ambulance, Royal Army Medical Corps, retrieve the 'wounded' from the scene of a vehicle 'ambush' during an exercise in Germany. The ambulance version can carry four stretcher patients or two stretcher and five seated casualties.
32. The FV432 is used by the Royal Engineers to carry the EMI Ranger anti-personnel minelaying system. The latter comprises 1,296 mines which are ejected to a maximum range of 140m, forming an instant minefield.

▲ 33

33. Ranger is often employed to cover anti-tank minefields in order to hinder their clearance. The anti-tank mines are laid by the mechanical Bar Minelayer towed behind an FV432 which, with a constant supply, can lay up to 600 mines per hour.

34. As a counter to minefields, the Royal Engineers use Giant Viper. It comprises a 250m-long hose fitted with 1½ tons of plastic explosives that is rocket-propelled across a minefield and detonated, resulting in a partially clear lane 200m long and 8m wide.

35. A further counter to mines, and one often used in conjunction with Giant Viper, is the Mine Plough, which rakes the ground

ahead of the vehicle, lifting mines to each side. In the British Army the device is mounted on the Centurion AVREs and Chieftain AVLBs of the Royal Engineers, but it can also be fitted to MBTs.

36. The Centurion has been in service with the British Army for forty years and will remain so in various specialized guises until the next century. The Royal Engineers employ two versions of the Centurion AVRE; the 165 armed with a 165mm demolition gun and the 105 armed with the standard L7A1 tank gun. Here an AVRE 165 makes short work of demolishing an old hut with its front-mounted dozer blade.

▼ 34

35▲   36▼

37. The FV180 Combat Engineer Tractor (CET) is purpose-built for the Sappers and specifically designed to provide integral engineer support for the battle-group. Weighing 17 tons fully loaded, CET combines good earth-moving performance with high cross-country mobility.

38. The CET can be driven forwards or backwards with equal facility by its two-man crew. When reversing it functions as an earth-mover, with an output comparable to that of a medium crawler tractor such as a Caterpillar D6C. The FV180 can tow trailers (here shown with Giant Viper) and items of construction plant up to 10 tons laden weight.

39. FV432 Armoured Personnel Carriers advance across country at speed during the course of an exercise attack. (Author)

40. An FV180 Combat Engineer Tractor digs a fire position for an MBT. (Author)

▲37   ▼38

▲41   ▼42

45. An FV18067 Land Rover Ambulance motors along a track at the British Army Training Unit Suffield (BATUS) in Canada.
46. A pair of 1-tonne Land Rovers of the Royal Signals pause during an exercise. (Author)
47, 48. The principal roles of the CET are the preparation and maintenance of operational routes, including the laying of trackway; the preparation of obstacles to impair the mobility of enemy forces; assistance to the battle-group in negotiating all obstacles, particularly across water; and the excavation of vehicle and gun pits for positional defensive operations.

47▲   48▼

▲49   ▼50

51▲

49. As an amphibious vehicle, CET acts as a pathfinder on water crossing operations, propelled by two rear-mounted water jet units. Its rocket-propelled anchor and hawser enable it to winch itself out of boggy ground or over high-sided river banks.

50. After many years of sterling service, the Ferret family of scout and armoured cars soldiers on in many roles, particularly that of liaison on the battlefield – in this case as an umpire's vehicle during a NATO exercise with the Danish Army.

51. The final version of Ferret was the Mk 5, armed with four Swingfire anti-tank guided weapons; one is seen here trundling through a German town. Although no longer in service with the British Army in this role, Ferret is widely used by many arms, especially by the Sappers for reconnaissance duties.

52. Soldiers of the Ulster Defence Regiment man a VCP (Vehicle Check Point) during a search operation; in the background is their Shorland Mk 3 armoured patrol car. Designed specifically to meet internal security requirements in Northern Ireland, the Shorland has been sold extensively abroad and is in service in 38 countries.

52▼

▲53 ▼54

53. The FV1611 Humber 1-ton APC was originally developed to meet a requirement for armoured personnel carriers during the Malayan Emergency. The majority were withdrawn from service in the mid-1960s, but with the deterioration of law and order in Northern Ireland many were recalled to duty and remain to this day as internal security vehicles carrying troops and stores over much of Ulster.

54. With the emergence of the terrorist bombing campaign in Northern Ireland, the Army responded with the development of a device known as Remote Handling Equipment (Tracked), EOD. Called more prosaically 'Wheelbarrow', it allows bomb-disposal technicians to inspect and disrupt suspect objects without endangering the operator. Illustrated here is the Mk 7 version.

55. Using the same chassis and automotive components as the FV432 APC, Abbot has been the mainstay of the field artillery for many years and follows in the Second World War tradition of naming self-propelled guns after ecclesiastics.

56. Abbot is armed with the L12A1 105mm gun in a fully rotating turret, with powered traverse and a maximum elevation of 70 degrees. Forty projectiles are carried, the maximum rate of fire is twelve rounds a minute, and the range is 17,000m.

57. A simplified version of Abbot, lacking such refinements as powered traverse and flotation screen, was developed for the Indian Army. Known as Value Engineered Abbot, one hundred were produced in the late 1960s and a few are in service with the British Army at BATUS in Canada, as shown here.

▲58

58. The M107 175mm self-propelled gun provides general artillery. support to the field army. It is crewed by thirteen members of the Royal Artillery and the vehicle has a range of 725km at a maximum speed of 54km/h.
59. Designed by the Pacific Car and Foundry Company, the M107 and the M110 share the same chassis and gun mountings. The

barrels are interchangeable.
60. The M107's 175mm gun fires only high-explosive rounds, to a maximum range of 32,700m. The projectile weighs 66.78kg and contains 13.6kg of TNT. The normal rate of fire is one round every two minutes.

▼59
60▶

▲ 61　▼ 62

63▲

◄64

61. An M110 8in self-propelled howitzer, the heaviest tube artillery piece in the Royal Artillery, is prepared for firing during an exercise in Germany. One M110 battery is attached to each division within BAOR.

62. With its earth anchor lowered for stability, an M110 of Ramsey's Troop, 39 Medium Regiment, Royal Artillery, fires on the Munsterlager Ranges in Germany.

63. The M110 can fire both nuclear-armed and conventional rounds, to a maximum range of 16,800m. Currently, both the M110 and the M107 are being refitted with a longer 8in barrel with a double-baffle muzzle brake, giving the redesignation M110A2.

64. The M109 155mm Self-Propelled Howitzer fills the gap between Abbot and the heavier M107/M110 series. It shares the same engine, giving it a top speed of 56km/h.

65. With a crew of six, comprising commander, gunner, three ammunition handlers and driver, the M109 provides full armour and NBC protection. Over 1,800 vehicles have been produced, by Bowen-McLaughlin-York of Pennsylvania.

66. An M109A1 of 45 Field Regiment, Royal Artillery, is prepared for firing at Hohne in West Germany. The M109A1 is an M109 fitted with a longer M185 barrel, an improved gunlaying system and a strengthened suspension.

▲ 65   ▼ 66

67. With a maximum elevation of 75 degrees, the M109A1 fires an HE shell to a range of 18,100m as compared to the 14,600m of the M109.

68. As a replacement for Abbot and M109, the Royal Artillery is likely to procure the tri-national SP-70, which uses the same weapon as the towed 155mm howitzer. The SP-70 is being developed by Britain, West Germany and Italy; illustrated is a first series prototype.

67 ▲   68 ▼

▲ 69

69. The heaviest weapon in the Royal Artillery, the Lance tactical guided missile system, comprises two tracked carrier vehicles; the one shown acts as the launcher for the missile, which is here being fitted with a warhead.

70. A Lance missile is prepared for firing aboard the M572 self-propelled launcher vehicle, which is a derivative of the M548 cargo carrier, itself a derivative of the M113 APC. (Author)

71. Ready to fire. The Lance surface-to-surface guided missile has a range of 120km and can be fitted with a variety of warheads.

▼ 70

71 ▶

▲72

72. Equally important to the Royal Artillery are towed weapons such as the FH-70 155mm field howitzer, which in the British Army replaced the venerable 5.5in gun of Second World War fame.
73. Produced jointly by Britain, West Germany and Italy, FH-70 is designated L121 by the Royal Artillery, who have procured 72 howitzers deployed in regiments of eighteen guns with six to a

battery. (Author)
74. The standard 4-ton truck of the British Army is the Bedford MK, here configured as a refueller. (Author)
75. A Foden (6×6) medium mobility vehicle with hydraulic crane being used as a gun tractor for a 155mm FH70 field howitzer. (Author)

▼73

▲76 ▼77

76. The latest general-service truck of the British Army is the Bedford TM 4-4 (4×4), which has a payload of 8,000kg. (Author)

77. A Foden (8×4) 22,500l Tanker of the Low-Mobility Load Carrier range moves across country. (Author)

78. A Chieftain MBT is refuelled from a Bulk Fuel Dispensing Unit mounted in a Stalwart Mk 2 High-Mobility Load Carrier. (Author)

79. The Scammell Crusader (6×4) Recovery Vehicle incorporates EKA D2030 B type recovery equipment which can also be utilized as a crane. (Author)

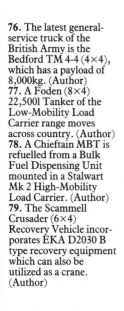

▲80　▼81

80. An AEC (6×6) Mk 3 Recovery Vehicle tows a Bedford RL 4-ton truck during a training session. (Author)

81. A Foden (8×4) LMLC with the Boughton Swap-body System unloads a flat-rack with Scorpion CVR(T). (Author)

82, 83. The British prime mover for the L121 field howitzer is the Foden 6×6 Gun Tractor based on the company's Medium Mobility Chassis. The vehicle features a removable cabin at the front, providing accommodation for the eight-man gun detachment. At the rear is a stowage locker for gun stores and equipment as well as up to four NATO 155mm ammunition pallets either side of the loading crane. (Author)

84. Entering service in 1974, the 105mm Light Gun uses the same ammunition as the Abbot SP gun. In the Royal Artillery each 105mm Light Gun regiment has three batteries of six guns each. The weapon proved highly effective during the Falklands War and has been exported to several countries. Here, three Light Guns fire at high elevation; at the extreme left is an L121 FH70.

82▲

83▲ 84▼

▲85　▼86

85. The standard infantry regiment employs a whole host of vehicles. Illustrated here with the Duke of Edinburgh's Royal Regiment is equipment ranging from an Austin 1800 Staff Car to an FV432 APC.

86. Designed as a highly mobile, all-terrain vehicle capable of being carried under light helicopter, Saboteur can be used for a variety of roles including ambulance, reconnaissance, logistic support and weapons platform. Two Saboteurs have undergone trials in the Falklands.

87▲ 88▼

87. Many armies are reassessing the military applications of the motorcycle. The current equipment in the British Army is the Can-Am 250cc Bombardier, as shown here with Royal Military Policemen of 111 Provost Company at Hohne in Germany.

88. First produced in quantity in 1948, the Land Rover has become ubiquitous throughout the British armed forces and, indeed, the world. Here, an LWB Land Rover (FFR) of the 1st Battalion, The Parachute Regiment, patrols along the inner German Border followed by a Ferret armoured car.

▲89 ▼90

52

89. A 109in long-wheelbase (LWB) Land Rover of the Commonwealth Monitoring Force in Zimbabwe prepares to move off on patrol. This vehicle is fitted with a sturdy roll-over bar and underfloor armour as protection against mines.

90. The ½-ton model Land Rover was designed to meet the special air-portable requirements of the British armed forces. Here, an air-portable (4×4) Land Rover tows a 105mm Light Gun out of a Luftwaffe CH-53G helicopter.

91. A pair of air-portable (4×4) 564kg Land Rovers (FFR) towing ¼-ton trailers lead a convoy of 1-tonne Land Rovers. FFR denotes Fitted For Radio.

92. The Centaur Multi-role Military Vehicle System designed by Laird (Anglesey) Ltd as a private venture combines the redoubtable Land Rover with the track of the Scorpion CVR(T) to give a low-cost, highly mobile load carrier or weapons platform. This Centaur is undergoing trials with the 17th/21st Lancers in Norway.

93. The 1-tonne Land Rover is used for a wide range of roles in the British army, and over 2,000 are in service. Production is now complete and the design concept has been adopted by Gomba Stonefield (left) for the world market. (Author)

91▲

92▲   93▼

94. The Royal Artillery employs the 1-tonne Land Rover as a prime-mover for the 105mm Light Gun and (as shown) the Rapier Air Defence System.

95. The standard 4-ton truck of the British Army since 1952, the Bedford RL remains in service with TA units and in specialized roles. With a container body on the back, this example is fitted out as a telecommunications maintenance workshop.

96. The successor to the RL is the Bedford MK (4×4) 4-tonne Cargo Truck, shown here in the standard configuration with the 27th Regiment, Royal Corps of Transport. Production of the 'M' series for both military and civilian use exceeds 36,000.

97. A Bedford MK (4×4) truck fitted with a snow plough takes part in Exercise 'Hard Fall' in Northern Norway, 1980. From April 1981, the designation changed from MK to MJ, 'MK' denoting a multi-fuel engine which has now been superseded by the 'J' diesel engine.

96 ▲   97 ▼

▲98 ▼99

98. A CH-47D Chinook medium-lift helicopter hovers over a Bedford MK 4-tonner to pick up pallets of fuel jerry-cans during an exercise in Belgium.

99. To aid the passage of wheeled vehicles over boggy ground such as river entry and exit points, the British Army employs Class 30 Trackway made from aluminium alloy planks and mounted on the rear of a Bedford MK. The 12m-long trackway can be laid in under ten minutes.

100. Trenches and field fortifications remain as important on the modern battlefield as ever, but today the task of producing these is expedited by such machines as the Light Mobile Digger. Based on a modified Thornycroft Nubian chassis, this can dig a trench 1.5m deep by 5m long in one minute.

101. In service since the 1950s, the Militant Mk 1 (6×6) 10-ton Cargo Truck is gradually being superseded by the LMLC (Low-Mobility Load Carrier) range of essentially commercial vehicles.

102. A Foden 8×4 LMLC prepares to move off with a 16-tonne cargo of palletized ammunition during an exercise at Liebenau, Germany, with the 1st Armoured Division Transport Regiment, RCT.

100 ▲

101 ▲ 102 ▼

▲103 ▼104

103. Petroleum operators check the amount of fuel in a Foden 8×4 22,500l tanker. Known as TTF (Truck Transport Fuel) 218 of the vehicles are in service with the British Army and the Royal Air Force.

104. Companion vehicle to the 8×4 TTF is the Foden 6×4 12,000l tanker, which is used by third- and fourth-line units in BAOR for the bulk transport of all types of fuels. A total of 199 are in service.

105▲ 106▼

105. Originally designed as a private-venture by Alvis Ltd using components of the Saladin and Saracen armoured vehicles, the Stalwart High-Mobility Load Carrier in the Mk 1 configuration as shown was introduced in 1961.

106. With a payload of some 5 tons, Stalwart has an excellent amphibious and cross-country capability, comparable to many tanks. Here a Stalwart Mk 2 (identifiable by the larger side windows) acts in its primary role as a front-line replenishment vehicle to armoured units, in this case the 5th Royal Inniskilling Dragoon Guards.

▲107

107. An FV432 of the 3rd Battalion, The Royal Regiment of Fusiliers, is replenished from Unit Bulk Refuelling Pods carried on a Stalwart Mk 2 at a rate of 50 gallons a minute. As there is no apparent successor for the ageing Stalwarts it is possible that the FV432 APCs replaced by MCV80s may be converted as armoured load carriers to fulfil the Stalwart role.

108. Another private venture that is likely to enter service with the British Army is the Alvis Stormer. Originally intended as an APC or MCV based on an enlarged Spartan chassis, Stormer is a contender as the carrier vehicle for Milan, HVM and Javelin in support of MCV80 battalions. (Author)

109. Produced by a consortium of West German companies, the M2 Amphibious bridging and ferry system entered service with the *Bundeswehr* in 1968 and with the British Army the following year. Here, an M2B of 28 Amphibious Engineer Regiment, Royal Engineers, moves out from its base at Hamelin in West Germany.

110. Sappers of 28 Amphibious Engineer Regiment, nicknamed the 'Rubber Ducks', manoeuvre M2B amphibious bridging vehicles into position to form a bridge over the Aller river, West Germany.

111. The Boughton Swap-body, or Ampliroll Mechanical and Hydraulic Loading-Lifting Equipment, here mounted on a Foden 8×4 LMLC, can exchange its cargoes or bodies, thus altering its logistic function. Here the Ampliroll swaps a Safety Fuel Tank for a flat-rack carrying a Scorpion CVR(T). The operation is carried out by the driver, alone and unaided, from the driving seat, in approximately three minutes.

▲108 ▼109

▲112

▲113 ▼114

112. A trio of AEC (6×6) Mk 3 Recovery Vehicles, Wheeled, Medium, pulls in concert to extricate a heavily bogged vehicle. The FV11044 AEC was developed in the 1960s as the replacement for the famous Scammell 'Knocker'/'Explorer' recovery vehicle.

113. An FV1119 Leyland (6×6) Recovery Vehicle Wheeled, Heavy, towing a low-loader, moves off to a recovery task in West Germany. The Leyland is capable of recovering on suspended tow all wheeled vehicles up to and including the 10-ton class.

114. The Scammell Crusader (6×4) Recovery Vehicle utilizes recovery equipment of Swedish Eka design to support wheeled vehicles up to the 16-tonne range on suspended tows or up to 40 tonnes gross with straight tows. (Author)

115, 116. Currently undergoing trials with the British Army as a replacement for the AEC and Leyland types is the Scammell S26 (6×6) Recovery Vehicle. It features both a slewing crane with a maximum lift capacity of 12,000kg (photograph 115) and the Eka support tow boom (116) shown here towing a Saracen APC over rough terrain.

115▲ 116▼

▲117 ▼118

119▲

117. With their commitment to guard the northern flanks of NATO, the Royal Marines employ the Volvo Bandvagn 202 tracked over-snow vehicle in a variety of roles, such as artillery prime-mover towing a 105mm Light Gun, mortar carrier, ambulance, command vehicle and radio vehicle. The BV202s operated by 407 Troop RCT proved invaluable during the Falklands War.
118. In service since 1969, the Eager Beaver rough terrain fork-lift tractor has been specifically designed to handle military loads in

difficult country. It can lift a maximum of 1,814kg.
119. For service in Norway and during inclement weather, an enclosed, heated cab can be fitted to the Eager Beaver, one of which is shown unloading Chieftain 120mm gun barrels.
120. An Eager Beaver Mk 2 loads ammunition boxes on to the rear-bed of a Stalwart Mk 2 HMLC. Powered by a Perkins 78bhp diesel engine, it has a top speed of 56km/h and can negotiate a 50 per cent gradient with a maximum load.

120▼

▲121   ▼122

123 ▲

21. The British Army currently has a requirement for approximately 1,000 rough-terrain material handling vehicles to replace its Eager Beavers. As an interim measure it has purchased a number of Mark Giraffe 342 Rough-Terrain Materials Handler vehicles. (Author)

22. Unlike Eager Beaver with its straight mast, Giraffe has its fork-lift mounted on a pivoted telescopic boom which gives a much improved placing capability. The Giraffe 342 has a lifting capacity of 2,870kg and can place a fully laden fuel pod weighing 2,360kg.

Here, a pod is being placed on the rear of a Bedford MK 4-tonner.
123. Originally designed by Thornycroft for oil pipe transport in the Middle East, the 'Mighty Antar' was adopted by the British Army as a tank transporter tractor to replace the wartime American Diamond T 980/981 M20 prime mover. Here, a section of Mk 2 Antars of 19 Company RASC parades in front of Diamond Ts.
124. An Abbot self-propelled gun claws its way up the ramps of an FV3011 50-tonne tank transporter semi-trailer with an Antar Mk 3 tractor up front.

124 ▼

67

▲125

▲126 ▼127

128▲

125. An Antar (6×4) Mk 3 tractor pulls an FV3011 semi-trailer cross M2B amphibious bridging vehicles spanning a river during an exercise in West Germany. The Antar Mk 3 has a redesigned cab, a new engine and transmission and many other improvements.

126. Despite the improvements to the 'Mighty Antar', it is inadequate to support the latest generation of MBTs such as Challenger, and so a new tank transporter train has been developed by Scammell. Known as Commander, this incorporates a version of the Rolls-Royce CV12 engine installed in Challenger. The British Army is procuring 125 Commanders; one is shown here with a Crane Fruehauf semi-trailer.

127. A Scammell Crusader (6×4) 35,000kg tractor tows a Craven Tasker 37-tonne RE semi-trailer carrying Sapper construction equipment through the West German town of Rinteln during

Exercise 'Spearpoint'. The 35,000kg tractor has a three-man cab with provision for two bunks.

128. The Sappers of the Corps of Royal Engineers undertake a multitude of tasks in support of the Army, both on the battlefield and behind the lines. Amongst these roles are road and route construction, building field fortifications and bridges, constructing landing strips and repairing airfields. To undertake these diverse jobs the Royal Engineers employ a wide range of construction equipment, some of which is illustrated in this and the next six photographs. This view is of a Michigan 275B Heavy Wheeled Tractor with its 5m³ capacity bucket used for airfield damage repair.

129. A Fiat-Allis Wheeled Loader fitted with a Class 30 trackway cradle.

129▼

130. An Allis-Chalmers Medium Wheeled Tractor, used for general earth-moving.
131. A Caterpillar D6C Dozer Medium Tracked Tractor. In this

131▲

photograph the vehicle is shown towing an 8m³ scraper.
132. A Caterpillar D8H Dozer Heavy Tractor used by the British Army for heavy earth-moving.

132▼

▲133

133. A Hymac Excavator 580BT (background), an Allis-Chalmers Medium Wheeled Tractor (left) and a Muir-Hill A5000 Light Wheeled Tractor with backhoe.

134. An Aveling-Barford Super MGH 12ft motorized grader.

▼134